Welcome!

I'm so glad you've joined me for this journey. As you work your way through recovery from spiritual abuse there are many areas to explore and process.

My hope is that this guided journal will give you a space to begin to process some of those areas. Perhaps, this will be a tool to start conversations with those in your life. Even still, this journal might serve as a guide as you process your trauma with a trusted therapist. I view this journal as a beginning point, a springboard, for the work ahead. The questions here are designed to serve as a starting point.

I encourage you to find a space that feels comfortable and safe. Grab a cup of something warm and soothing to drink and then dig in. If you begin to feel overwhelmed, take a break, and return when you feel ready.

Healing has no set time line so take as long as you need to work through this journal.

My hope is that in the days to come you will begin to find joy as you move toward a future filled with hope.

-Natalie

These are 10 things that bring me happiness no matter what kind of day I have had:

_____
_____
_____
_____
_____
_____
_____
_____
_____
_____

These are 2-3 people I can talk to if I feel overwhelmed:

_____
_____
_____
_____
_____
_____

Spiritual abuse can be difficult to define as it can take on many different forms.

Let's take a minute to consider some themes that are often seen in spiritually abusive places/relationships.

This is a list of some signs of spiritual abuse.
Notice which ones you have experienced:

In a spiritually abusive place someone (or sometimes many people within a system) take on the authority of God - to question them is to question God.

Religious texts are almost always weaponized to create an environment of fear and control.

Leaving the group is viewed in a negative way - sometimes even that you are straying from the faith

There is a different vocabulary that those outside the group or relationship would not understand

There is a skepticism of those outside the group sometimes a fear of them or belief that they are likely "lost" since they're not in the group

Performance or outward acts are praised and viewed as insight into your spiritual health - as a result, people are often judged as "backsliding" if they behave in certain ways

There is a need to conform in appearance and behavior

A lack of personal freedom

Beliefs are dogmatic - meaning there's little to no room for differing views/opinions

Often there is secrecy surrounding events/decisions that occur

Fear can be used by leadership to maintain some level of control over people's behavior

Other things I would add are:
_____
_____
_____

While viewing the list on the previous page I felt:

_____
_____
_____
_____
_____

I would describe the person or system that was spiritually abusive in this way to someone who never experienced it/them:

Freedom is not worth having if it does not include the freedom to make mistakes

Mahatma Gandhi

My earliest memory of the faith community where I grew up or my earliest memory of spiritual things:

_____
_____
_____
_____
_____
_____
_____
_____
_____
_____
_____
_____
_____
_____
_____
_____
_____
_____

Remembering that experience causes me to feel:

_____
_____
_____
_____
_____
_____
_____

Spiritual abuse is complicated.

We are going to take a look at how the spiritual abuse you endured affected your relationships with others as well as with yourself.

This is the earliest memory I have of feeling shame
due to my faith environment:

_____
_____
_____
_____
_____
_____
_____
_____
_____
_____
_____
_____

This is who (or what system) was responsible for triggering my shame and how that experience affected my relationship with them (or that system):

_____
_____
_____
_____
_____
_____
_____
_____
_____
_____
_____

A part of me was rejected by my faith community.
As a result I felt that I had to hide this part of myself:

I will take care of myself today by:
_____
_____
_____
_____
_____

The spiritual abuse I experienced resulted in me viewing people outside of our group in this way:

"When things change inside you, things change around you."
-Unknown

My family relationships were affected by the spiritual abuse I experienced in this way:

My friendships were affected by the spiritual abuse in this way:

The abusive environment/relationship affected my personality in this way:

While I was in the abusive system/relationship my view of God (Higher Power) was affected in this way:

_____
_____
_____
_____
_____
_____
_____
_____
_____
_____
_____
_____
_____
_____
_____
_____
_____
_____
_____
_____
_____
_____
_____
_____
_____
_____
_____
_____

Since I left the abusive system/relationship my view of God (Higher Power) has changed in this way:

The next few pages are going to explore the process of leaving the unhealthy relationship or environment.

If you are not yet at that point in your journey - **that's okay**!

Feel free to skip these questions or use the space to explore your fears or barriers to leaving.

Looking back on leaving the abusive relationship/environment this event or realization helped propel me to leave:

Now that I am removed from the abusive relationship/place I admire these traits I have because they helped me have the strength to leave:

_____
_____
_____
_____
_____
_____
_____
_____
_____
_____
_____
_____
_____
_____
_____
_____
_____
_____
_____
_____
_____
_____
_____
_____
_____

Now that I have left the abusive situation/relationship my relationships with family/friends are *still* being affected in this way:

_____
_____
_____
_____
_____
_____
_____
_____
_____
_____
_____
_____
_____
_____
_____
_____
_____
_____
_____
_____
_____
_____
_____
_____
_____

As I continue to move toward healing I hope to continue to grow in this area:

_____
_____
_____
_____
_____
_____
_____
_____
_____
_____
_____
_____
_____
_____

Moving forward from here I want to continue this work by:

_____
_____
_____
_____
_____
_____
_____
_____

CPSIA information can be obtained
at www.ICGtesting.com
Printed in the USA
BVHW051253240321
603339BV00011BA/1359